Shakespeare's Horse

Shakespeare's Horse

Joseph Harrison

WAYWISER

First published in 2015 by

THE WAYWISER PRESS

Christmas Cottage, Church Enstone, Chipping Norton, Oxon OX7 4NN, UK
P.O. Box 6205, Baltimore, MD 21206, USA
http://waywiser-press.com

Editor-in-Chief
Philip Hoy

Senior American Editor
Joseph Harrison

Associate Editors
Dora Malech | Eric McHenry | V. Penelope Pelizzon | Clive Watkins | Greg Williamson

Copyright © Joseph Harrison, 2015

The right of Joseph Harrison to be identified as the author of this work
has been asserted by him in accordance with the
Copyright, Designs and Patents Act of 1988.

All rights reserved

A CIP catalogue record for this book is available from the British Library

Pb ISBN 978-1-904130-77-2
Hb ISBN 978-1-904130-80-2

Printed and bound by
T. J. International Ltd., Padstow, Cornwall, PL28 8RW

Acknowledgments

I would like to thank the editors of the places where the following poems first appeared, sometimes in slightly different form.

The Antioch Review: "To Trebitsch Lincoln in Hell"

Arion: "To Riccardo Duranti," "To Barack Obama"

Birmingham Poetry Review: "Portrait of the Artist as a Young Kid"

The Common: "Henri Provence in Wessex"

The Hopkins Review: "Larkin's Nephew"

Measure: "King Lear"

The New Criterion: "Dr. Johnson Rolls Down a Hill"

nuovi argomenti: "To Quintus Minimus," "To Gallienus," "To Aeneas Silvius on Monte Amiata"

Parnassus: "Sky Burial," "Hearing Voices," "Hamlet"

Poetry Northwest: "The Key"

Poets.org: "Shakespeare's Horse"

Sewanee Theological Review: "Sparse Rhymes," "Damon"

Southwest Review: "To C"

Unsplendid.com: "The Place"

The Yale Review: "Fidelities," "Harrison's Clock"

I am grateful to the John Simon Guggenheim Memorial Foundation for a grant which was of great assistance in writing this book.

I would also like to acknowledge the following sources, to which individual poems in the book are deeply indebted: Walter Jackson Bate, *Samuel*

Acknowledgments

Johnson; Dava Sobel, *Longitude*; Colin Thubron, *To a Mountain in Tibet*; Bernard Wasserstein, *The Secret Lives of Trebitsch Lincoln*.

"We now stood in the Hidden Library of the Palacio Barolo. A familiar but not quite recognizable music was faintly audible. The rooms were all sizes, furnished in various styles, and their arrangement was odd: single rooms, sometimes quite large, led to suites of three connected rooms, which led in turn to another single room. When I asked the purpose of this design, my guide smiled. 'I wish I could remember whether I thought to put that question to Palanti while he was still alive,' he replied. 'But if I did, I don't recall his answer, if he answered at all. And even had he answered, I doubt he would have told me the truth, if he knew the truth.'"

– J. H. Hobson, *Six Days in Buenos Aires*

Contents

To C 13

✥

Windsock 16
To Pluto, Upon Its Declassification 18
Afghan Kites 21

✥

Wakefield 25

✥

To Quintus Minimus 33
To Gallienus 34
To Aeneas Silvius on Monte Amiata 35

✥

Dr. Johnson Rolls Down a Hill 38

✥

Henri Provence in Wessex 43
Larkin's Nephew 45
Oh 46

✥

Sunday Evening 48

✥

Contents

The Site 51
The Key 53
The Place 54

☦

Sparse Rhymes 58

☦

Archibald Leach 63
He Wasn't Proust 64
Portrait of the Artist as a Young Kid 66

☦

Damon 69

☦

To Riccardo Duranti 75
To Barack Obama 77
To His Book 79

☦

To Trebitsch Lincoln in Hell 81

☦

Sky Burial 94
Hearing Voices 96
King Lear 97

☦

Contents

Hamlet	99

✣

Ice Age Art	101
Fidelities	102
Harrison's Clock	105

✣

Shakespeare's Horse	113

To C

Let Dominica be the essence of green,
The florabundance of banana farms
With Sisserou and Jaco raiding the fruit,
Green birds, green fruit, green trees with massive leaves
Nodding in hillside waves at every breeze
That rolls in off the wild Sargasso sea
Accumulating mountainous evidence
Of afternoon's appointment with the rain,

And let the ochre dust of Roussillon
Signify the range of orange and red,
The rose and russet houses and placettes,
Sun-burned, eroded bluffs, and the dry air
Enveloping the hill-top sanctuaries
That overlook the windswept Luberon,
The painterly gradations that define
Light in the lavender summers of Provence,

And let the cobbled streets of Orvieto
Exemplify the purples and deep reds
Half visible beneath the gray patine
Now settled on blocchetti de porfido
Ascending toward the striped kaleidoscope,
The shimmering mosaic of facade
On the great Duomo, eclectic miracle
Perched on a tufa cliff in Umbria. . . .

In other lives we might have lived elsewhere,
Stunned by the carmine skyscapes of the west,
Or bundled tight against the polar cold
In crisp, astringent, boreal purity,
Or meditating in a bamboo hut
As sunrise floods the fields of Celebes,
Or listening to insects half the night
In fragrant torpor, drowsy and tropical,

To C

But here we are, in the middle of our lives,
In Baltimore, of all places, and satisfied
With modest comforts and a decent house,
Good friends, good food, and leisure to do as we please,
Even to travel for color, but coming home
To make our lives up in the airy dwelling
On into evening lightening with laughter
Where being here together is enough.

Windsock

This conical textile tube to show
   Wind direction and speed
      At sites with a need
         To know

(Airports, bridges, chemical plants)
   Senses, coming or going,
      Just what's blowing
         On, slants

To orient at about three
   Knots, extends at fifteen,
      Flutters between,
         Limps free

As it dies down, taking the measure
   Of elemental force,
      Or serves, of course,
         Our pleasure

In bright things that ripple and float
   For decorative show
      On patio
         Or boat,

Proving, if manufactured well,
   Something quite frail and slight,
      Set at a height,
         Can tell

Something essential about our world
   And, being empty, can fill
      Or fall, be still
         Or swirled

Windsock

In keeping with what's current, here
  And now (what, powerful,
    May whip, or lull,
      Or shear),

Can, flapping, indicate, if placed
  Domestically – just check
    The gimcrack deck –
      Our taste

In style and color (Santa, Seal,
  Pirate, Tropical Fish,
    Whatever you wish,
      Puce, teal),

But, *pace* ancestors in the Far
  East, where on high display
    Each Children's Day
      They star

As signs of luck, longevity
  And sons, streamlined and sharp
    Black and red carp
      At sea

In rushing air (some houses have none,
  Bitter end of the line),
    Cannot decline
      The pun

That finally whistles into place
  When blindingly, at last,
    The wind will blast
      Your face.

To Pluto, Upon Its Declassification

The word is out you're out, the ninth of nine
– Perhaps we wanted nine, like lives, or muses –
No longer. Fundamentals realign.
You've been unchosen as the new rule chooses,

"Declassified" by analytic tools
That say you're not the real thing, shown the door
Like doping medalists or discredited schools
Stripped of status for having rigged the score,

Dropped from the rolls, kicked off the podium,
Banished to outer rings of history
To orbit in perpetual odium
Or frigid wastes of pure obscurity,

Except you never committed any wrong.
You are the frozen sphere you always were
Before discovery, hurtling along
(Even in telescopes you're just a blur)

Your odd, elliptical trajectory,
"Highly eccentric," the same brown icy ball
Out in the Kuiper Belt's zone of debris,
Luminous for your size, but very small

By planetary standards, which apply
No longer. We'll redesign the orreries,
The planetaria. The naked eye
Won't miss you among all it never sees.

But will you miss the dazzling company,
Lavish, ambrosial, on Olympian heights,
Of Neptune, Jupiter, and Mercury,
Downgraded to hang out with lesser lights

To Pluto, Upon Its Declassification

Like Xena, Orcus, Makemake, Eris,
And Charon, your faithful, binary system moon?
How can a cosmic bum's rush not embarrass?
Who else will get reclassified? How soon?

And do we think such sleights of category
Will free us from dark thoughts of the underworld,
Of subterranean levorotatory
Landscapes where the murky waters, swirled

By deep rip tides, emit a noxious mist,
Where Sisyphus keeps slipping in the muck,
And scattered like brittle leaves, like windswept grist,
The darkling souls lament, eternally stuck

On the wrong side of Acheron or Styx?
The arguments are over, the die is cast
Like votes at a convention, and the fix
Approved, and in. You're out, no longer last,

And join the lengthening list of the demoted,
The cast off, airbrushed out, and sent back down,
The deanthologized, no longer noted
Inhabitants of Nowhere, a ghost town:

Ben Johnson, Harold Stassen, the Aral Sea,
Pomerania, Steam, Hanno the Great,
The mineral kingdom of taxonomy
And too many poets to enumerate,

Like Abraham Cowley, famous for being forgotten,
Once thought the peer of Milton, who admired him,
Whose "learned puerilities" and misbegotten
Pindaric cucumbers to what inspired him

To Pluto, Upon Its Declassification

Displayed his "lax and lawless versification,"
His negligence of diction, all the flaws
Exposed in Johnson's firm consideration,
Which exiled and preserved him. The harsh laws

Art yields to over time, massive attrition,
Survival of the fewest, raze and burn,
Position most of us in worse position.
Period pieces crack. The worm does turn,

While he still circles somewhere, scarcely read,
Tracing his faint ellipsis in the stark,
Chill nether regions of the all but dead,
Abysmal vacuums of Plutonian dark.

Afghan Kites

    Although
     At a first glance
   A visitor might think
  Them birds, or bits of colored paper
Spun by the wind in a tropospheric dance
 As far overhead they lift and sink,
   Curvet, dip, and caper
    As if by chance,
     This show

    Is not
    Just prettiness
   In curlicues of flight,
  Harmonic, terpsichorean,
But quick maneuvering under the stress
 Of an all-out aerial fight
   Combatants glory in,
    Asking finesse,
     A lot

    Of string,
    And racing will
   To dive and wheel full speed,
  Braving the endless, perfect blue
At altitudes of agonistic skill
 Where puffed-up boast succumbs to deed
  And weakness is cut through
   To pain or thrill
    (They sing

Afghan Kites

    Of that
     Day still). And these
   Frail artifacts of bright,
 Thin paper and whittled bamboo,
Far from mere brilliant toys crafted to please
 When unspooled to a dazzling height,
  Are framed and fashioned to,
    With wicked ease,
     Combat

    Both air
   And other kites,
  Across whose wires they slice
 Their own *tars* caked in an armored coat
Composing the edges of these scintillant fights
 (Adhesive, ground glass, and mushed rice)
  So, severed, off they float
   In pointless flights
    To where

   The street
   Boys run them down,
  Finders keepers, or "free
 And legal." The game plays when it can,
Catastrophe permitting, all over town,
 Defying mullahs who can't see
  ("Ban, ban, Taliban")
   Beyond their own
    Conceit.

Afghan Kites

    Intact,
     The sharp truth smarts:
    Beauty is ruthless, and
   It needs to be, given the at-
Mospherics and the odds, the moving parts
 (Whipping *tars* will ribbon a hand
   Or slit a throat, like that).
     Way off the charts
      The act

     Is still
     Appointed for
    Wind-hammered heights of play
   Both festival and hazardous,
As beauty and valor, air, pride, plume, and more
  Buckle in turn and are blown away,
    Whatever they meant to us
     Who knew the score,
       The kill.

✥

Wakefield

Start with the moral: the fabric of our lives,
Their texture of connection, from leitmotif
To puniest detail, the slipshod rooms,
The mismatched furniture, the slapdash walls,
Down to the knickknacks and the silly clock,
Is interwoven so precariously
One blunder, one fool act, one stupid word
Blurted in half-distracted thoughtlessness
Could be the casual tug on the causal thread
That starts the intricate tapestry of affection,
Allegiance, habit, comfort, and resolve
Unraveling. It dangles, beckoning
Some imp within us, curst, contrarian,
Some brat defying the parental "no"
To touch the hot plate, open the car door,
Let go the guiding hand and dart away
Into the perilous, concealing crowd,
Discovering the self in self-destruction.

Or uncovering its absence, for in fact
This is our queasiest, most nervous fear:
Our cultivated sense of who we are
Depends on simple ignorance of the weird,
Unruly laws that fashion identity
Through destinies as flippant as caprice.
We went to X not Y, we took the job
In Starkville, in an inexplicable funk
We broke it off, we opted to buy in
Two months before the firm went belly up.
These aren't the best examples; they contain
Traces of impulse or velleity.
The accident at the crosswalk, the cancelled flight,
The arsonist who moved in up the street,
These are our secret factors, the instruments

Wakefield

That seize our ends, rough-hew them how they will,
And strand us, outcasts of the universe.

Thus Wakefield, a man to all appearances
Vaguely unremarkable, middle-aged,
A little heavyset, of average height,
And though respectable not at all distinguished,
Afflicted by a certain sluggishness
One might mistake for mere complacency,
If intellectual just lazily so,
A bit too fond of some intoxicant,
And to those who knew him best, mainly his wife,
Displaying a trivial pleasure in deception
Giving the slightest hint what was to come:
One evening he left home on a short trip,
Purpose unspecified, and didn't return
For more than twenty years, when, out of the blue
(To be more accurate, out of the rain)
He simply showed back up, resumed his place,
And remained a regular husband until his death.

The reason for this hiatus? There wasn't one.
No mistress whose passion made his wife seem stale,
Whose amorous titillations led him off
Into a roller coaster pas de deux
Until she threw him out, or left, or died,
Or the thrill of the illicit wore away
Till what remained was tawdry, awkward, fraught
With recrimination and a dull regret
That made him long for everything he'd spurned,
His fireside, books, and rocker, and a wife
Whose placid toleration calmed his nerves.
No secret crime he vanished to conceal
Or spend the fruits of, till the long entr'acte
Elapsed without discovery, or the few

Wakefield

Cognizant of his fraud had passed away,
Persuading him the coast was finally clear.
No accident that left the man confused
And injured, isolated in a town
Where no one knew who he was or especially cared,
Until, years later, some erratic spark,
A smell, a voice, the mention of a place
Ignited a synapse, and point by point his world
Swam back into focus, like a metropolis
Minute by minute emerging from a fog,
The street lamps, sidewalks, doorways, finials
Gradually clarifying, and, still dazed,
Half-blind in sudden sunlight, he knew his way
Back to his distant harbor, if not his name.

As it turned out, he hadn't even left town,
Just rented a flat in an adjacent street,
Planning, at first, only the briefest stay,
A break from habitude, to clear his mind,
And also, maybe, to unnerve his wife,
So self-assured in her sedate routine.
But this odd, momentary interruption
Gathered a drift and purpose of its own,
Seemed to acquire its own strange lassitude,
Its own inertia settling in for good.
So days turned into weeks, weeks into years.
He grew a beard and whiskers, altered his dress,
Adopting a shabbier, bohemian style,
Spoke with a trace of accent, found new haunts,
Took different work under a different name
And reveled in the dark, elaborate joke
Of having vanished under everyone's nose,
Till even his pleasure in that seemed nothing more
Than fantasies of someone else's life.

Wakefield

To pull this off at close proximity
Was possible only in a teeming hive
Like London, swarming with humanity
And the intimate anonymity of crowds.
Everyone looks like someone, or so they say.
He didn't even avoid his former house,
But almost daily would slink past the spot,
Though always on the other side of the street,
Protected from detection by carriages,
Pedestrians, and a row of sickly trees.
He watched his wife, first shaken, then in black,
Plod on about her errands as in a dream,
Witnessed her slow recovery, her descent
Into a dull, autumnal loneliness.
And sometimes, in the evening, he beheld
Her shadow cast by firelight, her nose and chin
Distorted in dancing, flickering grotesque,
Like some old witch of folklore, up from the depths.
But eventually these skulking visitations
Grew more infrequent, then stopped, having come to seem
A pointless repetition, a return
To something no longer even a little strange.

One evening, quite by accident, he found
Himself outside the old place, lost in thought.
It had been one of those dour London days
When steel-gray storm clouds blanket a sunless sky,
Listless and motionless, holding the threat
Of a thorough soaking over everyone's head
With occasional passing splatters, but holding off
Till it darkens a little too quickly as the wind
Picks up the jettisoned papers, the trees sway,
The awnings flap, the atmosphere heaves and shudders
And a drumroll announces the collisional boom
As all hell breaks loose, pounding the cobblestones

Wakefield

At narrowing angles, streaming the windowpanes
And flooding the gutters, the world is aslant and awash
And drenched to the shivering bone, and Wakefield, jolted
Into the present moment, recognizes
The firelight caressing the parlor window, and sees,
In a flash, himself as that ludicrous thing, a man
Lacking the sense to come in out of the rain,
And in a surge of whimsy ascends the stairs,
Raps the familiar knocker, and enters his home.

Or so Nathaniel Hawthorne figured it,
Pondering the story in his little room
Under the eaves, the "dismal and squalid chamber"
Where he labored in painful anonymity.
Fanshawe a failure he was so ashamed of
He'd thrown his only copy on the fire,
How could he stand it? What was he waiting for?
His mother and sisters, quietly, downstairs,
Took most of their meals apart, not to disturb
The fledgling artist's curious agony.
Would it be possible simply to walk away,
To disappear in Boston, or New York,
Or even, perhaps, in London, and disavow
A life that had narrowed to too blunt a point?
Promise, ambition, expectation, trust:
These are the stuff of nightmare, not of dreams.
Imagining Wakefield he could almost conceive
The man he might become if he let go
And let himself go under, slipping down
The decomposing shifts of solitude.

I understand, I think. For several months
I've been in London on sabbatical,
In a small, walk-up flat in Belsize Park,
Working, in theory, on another book.

Wakefield

I've got my Pakistani takeaway,
My well-worn pub, my corner for cake and tea.
Hardly a thing gets written, but no one minds.
I don't think about my colleagues, who strike me
As absurdly self-important, painfully dull
In all the ways some academics are,
Absorbed in the utter trivialities
Of vicious internecine plots and coups.
And if for a while I thought about my wife
That's lessening, and I am fine without
Her cavalcade of fresh anxieties,
Imagined faux pas, timorous protocols,
And need to redecorate something every week.
There I exaggerate, but not by much.
I love my wife, or did, perhaps do still,
Just not as much as I love having nothing to do
But sit and read without taking a single note,
And forget what I was thinking, or what I am:
A minor talent who didn't live up to that.

But that's all past. Arrangements have been made
To transfer funds to an off-shore account.
It isn't a fortune, but it will be enough.
I've taken another flat, I won't say where.
When my flight leaves tomorrow I won't be on it.
My colleagues will feel self-righteously justified,
Having long thought me "unprofessional,"
A label I've always embraced, to their chagrin.
My wife will be bewildered and, yes, hurt,
Or her pride will be, but she will quickly find,
Being attractive, wealthy, and a flirt,
A man who is better suited for soirees
And fundraisers, and will take a livelier interest
In the politics of arranging dinner parties.
No one will miss me much, I'm relieved to say,

Wakefield

And I won't miss me either, as I was.
I think I'll read all of Trollope, then do it again.
I've finished the final meal I'll put on this card:
Bone marrow and parsley salad, which was superb,
Followed by saddle of rabbit with butterbeans,
Accompanied by Châteauneuf-du-Pape
And rounded off with a sip of Courvoisier.
All that remains is to settle up the bill,
Return to my rental, pack, and finish this,
The very last poem you'll ever have from me.

✥

To Quintus Minimus

Catullus cxvii

May all the vulnerable young
Steer clear of you, Quintus, you scoundrel
Hounding the helpless, you brow-beating
Pedant, sticking your stupid
Opinions all over their poems.

To Gallienus

"He was a master of several curious but useless sciences, a ready orator, and elegant poet, a skilful gardener, an excellent cook, and a most contemptible prince."– Gibbon

Gallienus, buried under centuries
Of opprobrium for your pompous inattention
   As the empire veered into chaos,
   Shrugging off invasions
   And plagues with a quotable quip,
Roused, when roused at all, to punitive cruelties,
Slaughtering young and old throughout Illyricum,

You total disaster (though a talented fellow,
Master of sciences curious but useless,
   Well-spoken and good in the kitchen,
   Reciting elegant poetry
   At ridiculous banquets, and doing
Whomever wherever, who blew off a crisis
Considering esoterica with Plotinus),

What, really, could *you* have done, with thirty tyrants,
Franks in Galicia, Goths in Ephesus,
   The Suevi with their hair-knots
   Crossing the Alps, and your father,
   Worthy Valerian,
Skinned and stuffed with straw and hauled about
In hideous effigy? Repress it all.

Who needs the linen of Egypt, the arras of Gaul?

To Aeneas Silvius on Monte Amiata

"In the cool air of the hills, among the old oaks and chestnuts, on the green meadow where there were no thorns to wound the feet, and no snakes or insects to hurt or annoy, the Pope passed days of unclouded happiness."– Burkhardt

Ambitious worldling, ubiquitous diplomat,
Adept at shifting sides a little faster
Than turns of Fortune's wheel, perfecting that
Leap from the falling to the rising master,
Imperial laureate, reluctant pastor,
Backroom maneuverer with sufficient skill
To supersede Guillaume d'Estouteville,

For whom taking orders was relinquishing
Venus for Bacchus, who matured to be
"The man who had a heart for everything,"
From nature, doctrine, art, cosmography,
And ruined riddles of antiquity
To boat races and feasts, shrewd city planner,
Suasive orator in the classic manner,

You sired two bastards, true, when young, and wrote
A smutty literary curio,
But on deliverance from a storm-tossed boat
Piously, though the path was frozen slow,
Walked ten miles barefoot through the ice and snow
To pray at the nearest shrine, as you had vowed,
And suffered pain thereafter, though not aloud.

Diverse Piccolomini, Renaissance man
Before Castiglione or *The Prince*,
Or rising anti-Trinitarian
Disturbances, or Leonardo's tints
Teasing our gaze for meaning ever since,
Having, on elevation, set to work
Against Catilinarians and the Turk

To Aeneas Silvius on Monte Amiata

With Quattrocento clarity, what relief,
Despite intrigues and venomous ill wills
And plans for coalition come to grief,
Plus torment from the gout, and other ills,
Carried by litter over the Tuscan hills,
You felt at ease in Amiata's shade
Beneath chestnuts and oaks, where sunlight played

Tricks of perspective on the studious eye
Marking beyond the steep declivity
Siena's towers against the cobalt sky
(You couldn't climb up to the top to see
Distant Sardinia lifting off the sea),
Finding yourself, peaceful against all hope,
That contradictory thing, a happy Pope.

Dr. Johnson Rolls Down a Hill

Even a man of voluminous gravity,
The monumental lexicographer
Who labored in inconvenience and distraction,
In sorrow, sickness, and slovenly poverty
Unaided by the learned or the great,
A man of girth and passionate appetite
Who relished with dispatch and enormous zest
Huge stacks of pancakes, bottomless pots of tea,
Along with whatever conversational thrust
Kept the mind nimble and the spirit light,
Delaying the final, agonizing hour
When he lumbered off to bed, always alone,
To self-recrimination in pitch dark,
Contains in his heart of hearts a little boy
Who played and played all day, without a thought
Of duty or expectation or penury
Or wasted years diminishing all the time.

Not to idealize childhood, least of all his:
Barely alive at birth, too weak to cry,
Infected in infancy by tubercular milk,
Rendered half blind, half deaf, with an open wound
Stitched in his little arm for his first six years
(An issue, with so much else, he learned to ignore),
Scarred by the scrofula, and further scarred
By being cut sans anesthesia,
He wasn't a pretty sight, but bore it all,
The constant pain, the perpetual awkwardness,
The fretting of parents, and the feckless taunts
Of boys who could play ball and ridicule
The rawboned, driveling prodigy in their midst,
And grew to be a man of great physical strength
Despite his pitiful incapacities.

Dr. Johnson Rolls Down a Hill

The body had its struggles. So did the mind.
The photographic memory, the sheer
Celerity and clarity and taut
Engagement with the question, small or large,
Be it some pressing affair of state, or some
Domestic crisis pressing upon the heart
Of one he loved, encompassing his point
With honesty and syntax and good sense,
Such gifts the mind deployed with bravery
While poised above a vertiginous abyss
Opening wide within, a whirligig
Of deep afflictions and anxieties:
Depression, sloth, despair, paralysis,
An "inward hostility against himself"
In which his massive critical faculty
Would pulverize his puny self-regard,
And, worst of all, pure terror at the dark
Encroachments of what seemed insanity.

Now, in his middle fifties, the shadows lengthen,
"A kind of strange oblivion" overspreads him.
Beset by horrors and perplexities,
The clicks and spasms and clucking of Tourette's
Markedly worsen as the great man sinks
Deeper in torpor, till guilt at time misspent
Freezes and harrows him, transfixed, become
A spectator at his own stunned debacle,
Tortured by scruples like pebbles in his shoes.
He's written nothing for years, and Shakespeare waits,
Promised and paid for but beyond him still
(What infinite riches, and what little room),
As vast resources of intelligence
Fritter away from faulty "character,"
And reason flickers, dying, all but snuffed
Out by the listless drift of hopelessness.

Dr. Johnson Rolls Down a Hill

His friends try to distract him, to little avail,
With a club, a trip to the country, anything. . . .

He visits Lincolnshire with Bennet Langton
In January 1764.
He's on his best behavior, charming both
His young friend's parents and their visitors.
One fine, dry afternoon, windless and clear,
They set out walking on the Lincolnshire wolds.
Only the groundsel's in bloom, a tentative yellow,
As they amble past tufts of grouse scrub, furze, and thorn,
But the air has a pleasing crispness, with a rich,
Effluvial hint of leaf-mold or of wood-rot.
The hills are varied by streaks of yellowish red
Which vaguely correspond to, lower down,
The low, red roofs of occasional cottages.
Everything's very still. There are just three birds:
A fluttering brace of fieldfares (or are they redwings?),
Plus a lone kestrel, hovering for a vole.

They reach the top of an impressive hill.
Admiring its steepness, suddenly Johnson declares
He has "not had a roll for a long time."
Against the objections of the company
He divests himself of pencil, keys, and purse,
Lies down at the edge, and, after a turn
Or two, is off and tumbling and picking up speed
Flattening the flora in his path
While sending up puffs of chalk dust, now he's chuckling
As his weight propels him and his heaviness
Precipitating his new view revolves
As sky and earth wheel round in blue-brown circles
And happiness is merely being alive,

Dr. Johnson Rolls Down a Hill

As if the good life really were this easy,
As if the nightmare of his coming breakdown
Had no more substance than a child's bad dream.

Henri Provence in Wessex

Now, when the thatch-roofed cottages
  Send up their puffs and curls
From heating folk and pottages,
  And steadily thickening swirls

Of snow-feathers settle, limning
  Lintels and mullioned panes,
And door lanterns waver, dimming,
  And rusty weather vanes

Creak as they flip directions like
  Befuddled gyroscopes,
A chilling bleakness seems to strike
  Down all too human hopes

For what the year now past would bring
  And how our lives would change,
Before our goals for everything
  Had drifted out of range

(Time set aside for self-improvement
  Got taken up like slack;
The old inertias stymied movement;
  She never called you back).

When I, to see what prevents me,
  Go blundering outside,
The blank the winter presents me
  Scintillates far and wide

With all distinct articulation
  Of coppice, hedge, and heather
Erased in glazed disanimation
  By all-encasing weather

Henri Provence in Wessex

That levels whatever playing field
  We thought the game was on,
And levels us, who stand revealed
  As going, if not gone.

An influence presents itself
  Where all this absence is,
As if one old book on my shelf
  Inscribed precisely this,

As if down an empty country lane
  I saw Thomas Hardy go,
Ghosting the track of some whitened pain
  Like boot-prints filled by snow.

Larkin's Nephew

"I don't believe you're not on Facebook yet,"
    The bubbly poet said.
"I put everything up there, who I've met
    And where, what I've just read

Or had for lunch. People appreciate
    Knowing, they really do.
It helps us all keep so in touch – it's great!
    It'd work real well for you.

All your old friends could find you then, from high
    School, right on line. You never
Know who might pop up next and just say 'hi.'
    It's like the best thing ever."

Somehow I'm not persuaded. It makes less sense
    To let the great net work
If you're like me. Flashbacks to adolescence?
    To times I was a jerk

Playing elaborate jokes on some dumb schmuck
    Who never stood a chance?
That guy might track me down now – just my luck.
    My hot date to the dance?

I didn't have one, ever. Can't I please
    Keep on forgetting years
Sullied by acne and anxiety's
    Clammy pubescent fears?

I will admit I've sometimes been curious
    What happened to two or three
Young women on whom my crush was furious.
    But they never cared for me.

Oh

When Love herself came to me
Framed by the classroom door
Her presence shot straight through me,
My heart dropped to the floor.

Nothing phantasmal slew me.
What eyes and hair and skin
Could do they did to do me,
Helpless and hopeless, in.

Oh when her news came to me
– Ovarian, forty-four –
Her absence echoed through me,
Ringing my hollowed core.

Sunday Evening

The night is clear, without the slightest wind,
As the moon poses her soft white proposition
Above the plaza and the rooftop gardens.
Even the mountains are visible on the horizon
As jagged pieces sliced from the rim of the sky.
Sweetheart, the streets are quiet, a few windows
Reflect the lives still taking place by lamplight
Or the blue flickering of a television.
You are asleep now, in your chic apartment,
Perhaps alone, perhaps not, having cancelled,
Politely but firmly, our long awaited evening,
Pleading fatigue. And last night *was* a party.
I'd say you looked your best, but every time
I think you do the next time you look better,
Which makes things worse, and worse they may be yet,
For who's to say your best's not still to come?
Not me, who hope I won't be there to see it
And pray I will, or all those other fellows
Who cleverly compete for your attention
While I observe your triumph from a distance
Across the room that might be miles, or years.

Speaking of years, who now reads Leopardi,
Or Keats, or Shelley, or even Wallace Stevens?
You used to. Now you haven't got the time,
And I can't say I blame you. They're not changing.
What's new is fast and all the buzz and edgy.
What, really, is the point of antique passions
– An oxymoron if there ever was one –
Except to pluck the classical guitar strings
Of melancholics' overripe nostalgias?
Names that once conjured worlds mean little today.
The evening's silence seems a comment on them
Like lapses in attention, and if a poem
Somebody wrote two hundred years ago

Sunday Evening

Informs the space your absence opens here
(It stretches all the way to Recanati)
Would anybody know unless I told them?
And now the silence suddenly gets broken,
Ruptured by woofers, and an engine revving,
And high-heeled, tipsy laughter clacking home,
Sounds sharpening the ache of the outsider
Who hears the young world rushing on without him.

When I was a little boy in Alabama
I used to lie awake on Sunday evenings.
The weekend I had waited for was over,
And why was I so sad? The Fifth Dimension
Sang somewhere on a crackling radio
About the dawning age of constellations
Or something. I couldn't tell. But I did know
There was some big thing happening without me
And I would always live with having missed it.
I was born just too late, and missed the Sixties,
Though not the sense the world had changed completely
In ways I couldn't wrap my head around
That somehow got embodied in the music.
I didn't know why what I felt inside me
Tugged and tangled and wound itself up into
A giant knot of unrelieved frustration
So dolorous I sobbed into my pillow.
The dull school days ahead (I hated school),
Insipid as institutional architecture,
Kept stretching off as far as I could see.
I knew the music hurt me. It still does,
Dying off bit by bit in memory,
Even tonight, at my age, to the core.

✢

The Site

Welcome to the site. There is no need
For you to furnish personal information,
Financial or otherwise. We have all that
Already in your file, which activated
The moment you logged on, and contains, as well,
Full documentation of errors you've long forgotten,
Early embarrassments, rank ineptitudes
You've wiped your record clean of, but not ours,
Humiliations suffered and meted out,
Crass self-indulgence, curt ingratitude,
The outright frauds, the sinuous lies left in,
All catalogued, were there reason to produce
Evidence in the course of these proceedings.

Cooperation is, you will admit,
The best route, not to say the only one.
You have a simple password now required
For everything. To form it, just insert
Your name and date of birth into the code
"JohnDoe060666thefool."
Should you ever be forced to leave your screen
For longer than the standard daily allowance
(Three twenty-minute breaks, six hours at night)
By medical emergency or fire,
Or receive a privilege day of personal leave
To attend a funeral or consult a surgeon,
You'll need it to log back on and resume your life.

Here is your list of friends. A few you know,
A few know you, most of them we've selected
Using compatibility algorithms.
Here is your pictorial representation,
The eyes, the hair, the smile by which you'll be
Identified as you from this day forward.
Better, you must admit, than you as you were,

The Site

And all who love you will be happy you
Look as they could have wished you all along.
We trust you will not fail to recognize
This altogether flattering transformation
As one more reason not to leave your screen.

Not that you'll ever want to. Virtually
Every form of entertainment is here
At finger-tip control: travel the world
To jungle, reef, savannah, glacial peak
Swept over in 3D, with background music
From our extensive . . . well, you get the picture.
Plus videos, movies, concerts, galleries, sports,
Books graphic and otherwise, perpetual parties,
Family reunions, all here: just see the menu.
And the games, of course. The games go on and on,
Fast and violent all the way up the ladder
And ratcheting effects to boost you again.
We've signed you up for all the latest versions.

These are the only available arrangements.
You understand, we think. Of course. We thought so.
Deactivate your will with just a keystroke.

The Key

Here is the key. The lock is on the door
Of a small cabin in a distant wood
Standing for something you've never understood,
An emptiness that's full of metaphor.

Assembly *is* required. Don't mind the score,
It's minding you. You might have known it would
Be all attention, taking your measure for good
Like the complaining boards of a warping floor.

The key's in your pocket, hot as the summer sky
Baking the city you left years ago.
The streets forgot your absence, by and by.

Here it's darkening. Soon it's going to snow.
Then the brilliant cover, the perfect lie
Telling what little truth you've come to know.

The Place

You'll never find the place, but you must try.
Start on a rain-lashed, storm-tormented night,
Driven by gusts and gales in stark-blind flight
(Instructions for navigation are a lie).
Come day, the landscape gives you the evil eye
From every angle's freshly hideous sight

Of blasted, strip-mined hillsides, curdled pools
Radiating an unnatural sheen
From surfaces of foam-fringed, toxic green.
A foul smell drifts in noxious molecules.
What dismal game, played by what dirty rules,
Contrived to bring you to this blistered scene,

Dragging your damaged sensibility
To what bad end? A permanent eclipse,
Whether it's pre- or post-apocalypse,
Surrounding you as far as you can see
In random mounds of dirt, gravel, and scree,
Of what you thought the world was? The worst trips

Of nightmare, or psychedelia gone wrong,
Were larks compared to this infernal fix.
The lines of dead trees stand like burnt matchsticks
Up the next valley, where you trudge along
The brown, cracked dryness of a billabong.
The very ground, like malformed cicatrix,

Looks traumatized, infected. You push on
To climb, at last, onto a barren plain
(What bitter labor for what dubious gain)
Of gray cement. What engineers, long gone,
Laid out this space from which all life's withdrawn?
What overlords required such dead domain?

The Place

A place without inflection, ornament,
Or variation: every inch the same,
Now nameless, if there even was a name
For all its single-minded bleak intent.
What creatures lived here dully came and went
Without a remnant, if they ever came.

And yet you cross it, somehow, to arrive
At a vast tract of ugly, uniform
Apartment buildings. Whatever spies inform
The premises, not one thing seems alive
In these dull eyesores ranged in groups of five,
Stuck in adherence to some stupid norm.

Beyond them, you encounter a huge mass
Of crushed, wrenched metal, twisted, tortured piles
Of scrap, abandoned, stretching on for miles,
All rust and wreckage. Crunching broken glass
You pick your way around each sharp impasse
To stagger on in search of other trials.

Waste land after waste land! And all man-made,
Or man-destroyed, civilization's crux
And crucible, matter itself redux
As pure detritus, while we masquerade
Pretending we were dealt the hand we played,
We who have seen the future, and it sucks.

Don't go there? How? Perverse euphoria,
To revel in such grand guignol grotesque,
Or scribble pornographic arabesque
To decorate phantasmagoria!
Social dementia's our aporia,
The end we've earned. For *this* you left your desk?

The Place

But in a flash the whole scene's morphed again:
There's grass, though withered, and a furtive stream
With a trickle or two of water, and what would seem
A clump of stunted trees, gnarled as in pain,
And hills (not mountains) ringing a little plain
Which looks familiar, maybe from a dream,

Or from a poem. Oh. This is the place.
Why didn't you, you old fool, recognize
Its round, squat truth against the ground of lies
You've crossed and recrossed, lugging the carapace
That can't protect you now? The prize you chase
Will turn on you and cut you down to size.

A bell tolls, once. You're back in time. You stand
Surrounded by a winding sheet of flame.
They see and know you, and you hear your name
Repeated mockingly, your corpus panned
As failed at failure, who crashed *Alastor*, and
Who blew "'Childe Roland to the Dark Tower Came.'"

Sparse Rhymes

"O poverella mia, come se' rozza!"

    When I was a young man
    I was like a little child
Who, desperate to speak, has not yet learned
        To make the sounds he can
        Hear, and it drives him wild.
Frustrated, flummoxed, I kept on getting burned
        Whenever the urge returned
        To finally be heard,
        The heart on my sleeve a joke
        Your laughter sent up in smoke,
My stammers marring every perfect word,
        My tongue just in the way
        Of all I tried to say.

    When I at least attained
    A basic fluency
I thought you'd love me. Every undertaking
        Set out with mind's eye trained
        On your eyes fixed on me,
Not on the road straight uphill I was taking.
        I was, of course, mistaking
        Your interest all the time
        In what could only bore,
        My stiff attempts to score
With reams of thudding rhythm, gorgeous rhyme.
        For proof I was deluded
        Reality intruded

Sparse Rhymes

   As your demurrals came
   Rocketing back by post.
I wasn't, really, someone *you* could date,
     Recipient of a name
     Rejected coast to coast,
The late beginner who began too late.
     Call it bad luck, or fate,
     Or instrumental flaw:
     Although I felt maligned
     (Your notes weren't even signed),
Selection picks. The law is just the law.
     Dislike is natural
     Where love's ephemeral.

   And when I turned more hip
   (Farewell academy,
Hello café: why *not* performance art?)
     You still gave me the slip
     With deft celerity.
I conned myself into another part:
     You, prompted, broke my heart
     Along with our appointment,
     Infinite expectation
     Just hallucination.
The gadget broke, the fly stuck in the ointment
     As yet another stage
     Got flattened by the page.

Sparse Rhymes

    As someone bad at poker
    Who keeps on losing hands
Will once, right when he needs it, draw the ace
      (Or was it just the joker?)
      He hardly understands
Will serve to keep him, losing, in his place,
        One time I saw your face
        And you *did* smile. I'd scored
        Big, in the nick of time
        The cards lined up like rhyme
And here you came, and out my winnings poured
        In brilliant, brief success
        That paid off less and less.

    You long since stripped me clean.
    These days my instrument
Makes harsh sounds only, as befits my age.
      I shrink from anything green
      And full of all that meant,
The hearts on ice, the diamond equipage.
        At my diminished stage
        I simply watch you stroll,
        As if the world were yours
        For parties and grand tours,
Out with the latest stylist on a roll,
        Or sometimes, down by the water,
        Playing with your daughter,

Sparse Rhymes

    Reminding me of . . . no.
    We'll leave some things unsaid.
Inside a place we called the Forest of Arden
    We walked once, long ago.
    You barely moved your head,
Your voice was faint, you vaguely begged my pardon.
    I felt my proud heart harden.
    So it went, and always would.
    What rhymes I have I scatter
    Wherever they least matter,
Here where we walked that evening. If I could
    I'd sing you one last song
    But fear I'd get it wrong.

    Little song, you know you're no good.
    Better stay here in the wood.

Archibald Leach

Archibald Leach was the perfect leading man
Who had that *je ne sais quoi* you can't teach.
His dapper smarts and rapid-fire élan
Were signature, but not signed Archibald Leach.

Men mimicked his clip and polish. To the girls
He was dreamy as ice cream sundaes at the beach.
But who, adoring his picture, reciting his pearls,
Knew that the man with that view was Archibald Leach?

Granted he carried the day, whatever the name
Considered for awards just out of reach.
The credits keep on rolling just the same.
But credit is never given to Archibald Leach.

He Wasn't Proust

In London, on his birthday, he went to a play
That seemed a good bet: Helen Mirren in *Phèdre*.
He thought it unlikely he would be disappointed,
Or crushed if he were: he wasn't Marcel Proust.
And this was no reprise – for her the role was new.
What were the chances *she* would be underpowered?

But her performance was, well, underpowered.
Though he was rather impressed with the rest of the play,
The staging, the acting, even the verse, he knew
Its star had fallen short (too old for *Phèdre*?),
Straining, like an aging character in Proust,
At a forced passion. Mildly disappointed,

He was disturbed he wasn't more disappointed.
His own reaction was, well, underpowered.
Why couldn't he, like young Marcel in Proust,
Feel crucified by art? At his first play,
Anticipating his favorite part of *Phèdre*,
When "Berma" would sound the deepest speech he knew,

"On dit qu'un prompt départ vous éloigne de nous,"
He was so devastatingly disappointed!
His dream of dreams, to see "Berma" as Phèdre,
Was ruined: her voice was flat and underpowered.
He didn't have the experience of the play
He'd always imagined. He was already Proust,

If years from being a character in Proust.
Perhaps all this would get *him* to write something new.
Not a sestina. For even when you play
Some high cards well, the reader is disappointed.
The teleutons turn mechanical, underpowered.
How many times can a poem mention *Phèdre*

He Wasn't Proust

And not be seeming to strain to work in "*Phèdre*"?
How many times can a poem bring up Proust?
On reflection, the whole idea seemed underpowered,
Thin, predictable, certainly nothing new.
Better not try at all than be disappointed.
So that was that. There was nothing to overplay,

Or under-. Powered down, and out, he knew
He wouldn't write about *Phèdre*. He wasn't Proust.
But he *was* disappointed, though not with the play.

Portrait of the Artist as a Young Kid

There they were in the basement, the whole troop
   Of Cub Scouts, including his brothers,
   Instructed by attending mothers
In projects spread out on the ping-pong table
   Right at eye level (he was five
      And out of the loop),
   Where he could, barely, see
   A jumbled activity
    He was unable
To join line up and come alive,
As each initiate was shown
How to fold a Reader's Digest into a cone,
   Which soon, spray-painted green
   Then sprinkled with glitter and cotton strands
(And just like that somebody's life expands:
   Was this the coolest thing he'd seen?),
     Emerged from their clumsy hands
      A Christmas tree.
    What strange, imagined lands,
     What inner sea

Right then conceived their dark geography
   And left the issued world behind,
   Their black maps rising in his mind?
What territories, perilous and wild,
   Whose powers would demand oblation,
     Then came to be,
    In firmaments apart,
    The regions of his heart?
     The scheming child
   (Always beyond representation)
   Had a vague notion what to do:
He made, with cotton balls and Elmer's glue,
   A shapeless pile of gloop
   Proudly affixing to the floor

Portrait of the Artist as a Young Kid

Off in a corner behind the basement door.
 So what he wasn't in the group?
  He'd seen what life was for
   And made a start.
  This thing was his, and more:
   It was his art.

Damon

"Go, for they call you, shepherd, from the hills."
Untie your charges, set their figures, penned
With all due caution for the present time,
Loose to consider what the signs intend
In fields of play star-dazzled, fringed with rime.
 They have their own free wills,
And they will wander, under a harvest moon,
Into predicaments you can't foresee
Where passages drop into history
Implicit in a word. Let it be soon.

Here, where some upland gardener planned the rows
And laid them out in, oh, two dozen plots
To make a statement through the sun and rain
With poppies, blue-bells, and forget-me-nots
(Whether such style will work this spot again
 Nobody living knows),
Here where the footing's tricky, the ground steep,
And no one comes now but the occasional poor
Student who can't tell what the place was for,
While most folk, docile, stay below, like sheep

But less adventurous, I sit and wait
To see what comes along. The view is quite
Romantic, one might say: the valley swerves
Down with the river's ribbon glinting light,
The hills stand forested in gentle curves,
 And though it's getting late
The trees still have their leaves, although they've turned
To rust and umber and alizarin
As cold, precise as clockwork, zeroes in
To teach them what their ancestors all learned,

Damon

A dyeing fall. Pencilled against the blue,
The Gothic spires of the academy
Compete with the church steeples of the town
For altitude and what antiquity
This stage set offers, till the sun draws down
    The curtain, with much ado
Of lighting effects on a spectacular scale.
Till then, to pass time in this pastoral nook
I've bread, cheese, wine, and Matthew Arnold's book,
So I can read, once more, that wandering tale

Of the lone scholar who forsook his friends
And Oxford's citadel of inquiry
Along established lines, in scripted parts,
To choose a life of constant errancy
In search of ancient gnosis and dark arts
    For mesmerizing ends,
And disappeared into the landscape, hill
And field and tree turned signs of his vanishing,
His present absence, his self-banishing
In rigors of conjuration and wicked skill.

I know, my friend, what that poem brings to mind
For both of us: that character we knew
Some twenty years ago, when we were first
Trying to write more seriously, who
Would startle us with each rhapsodic burst.
    Fearless, one of a kind,
A learned enthusiast, a mad-cap bard,
He had entire anthologies by heart:
You couldn't stop him once you'd let him start.
His poems were densely coded, and too hard

Damon

For us to make much of. But we still thought
Something was going on there, for we heard
A different resonance, a pitch and key
Animating each encrypted word
With overtones of strange authority,
    Compelling and self-taught.
Try to advise him and he'd have none of it.
Tell him to let some air in, tone it down,
Just meet the reader halfway, he would frown
And scoff at compromise: he was above it.

He criticized *us*: we were stuck in time,
Attuned to the present moment, unaware
Of spectral pressures, unextinguished sparks
And ghostly demarcations, the very air
Swarming with presences, invisible marks
    At the scene of each new crime
Telling just whom we'd robbed. Our ignorance
Was no excuse. Trap doors in every trope
Dropped into the abyss. There was no hope
For dancers who couldn't sense the larger dance.

Then he was gone, dropped out of school and sight.
For a while we heard about him, knocking around,
Performing in cafés, or giving classes
In bookstore basements. Stories had him found
Haunting the alleys and the underpasses,
    A rag-tag anchorite
Reading to rats and winos. It wasn't pretty.
Soon he was homeless, living out of his car,
Strung out on dope, cracked up, locked up, or far
Gone down the vicious sinkhole of the city.

Damon

Or somehow he'd escaped his downward spiral.
He was squatting in a vacant barn in Sparks
And renting fishing boats on Pretty Boy.
He'd nabbed an airstream and was living in parks
In West Virginia. He was peddling soy
    Butter and antiviral
Herbal remedies on the Eastern Shore.
Now he was teaching yoga in Delaware.
He was all rumor, he was everywhere
And nowhere fast. Then we heard nothing more.

I do still think I see him, now and then.
On cliffs across the river at Great Falls,
Up a side street in Chelsea, walking fast,
As trains pull out of stations, at last calls,
When faces blend as crowds come pouring past
    I glimpse, time and again,
Reflections of who he was, or might be now,
Those deep-set gray-green eyes that look right through
Whatever public face you think is you
To size up just what you've become, and how.

At times I even think we made him up,
Or plucked some fellow out of history
To serve as foil and proxy, and explore
Precincts too marginal for you or me,
Beer stubes and rum dives of old Baltimore,
    To drain one final cup
Of some cheap, foul, nightmare-inducing stuff
And stagger off half-crazy, and then go
Roaming the streets with Edgar Allan Poe,
Agreed too much was never quite enough.

Damon

But that was life, or death. It was, of course,
In art that we admired his recklessness,
His upward swerving purpose, his conviction
That more was really more, and less just less,
His labyrinthine syntax, loaded diction,
    And fence-clearing high horse.
He knew the back trails through the mountain passes,
The sequences of all the trees and flowers,
Where caved-in grottoes were, and ruined towers.
He, clearly, saw it all. We wore dark glasses.

(Or blinkers. Was he right in getting out
Before it got to him, remaining pure-
Ly idiosyncratic? He didn't settle
For some entitled quasi-sinecure.
His touchstone leaves its mark on our cheap metal
    Dented by fear and doubt,
Security assured yet insecure.)
He's out there somewhere strange, insistently
Striding beyond reliance, cast off, free,
Trying to read the secretive signature

Of things to come, as in a glass reflected.
Spotting the cruise ships of the new regime
He fled the hoops and hoopla, traps and trends
And smug correction by the episteme,
Spurned colloquy and group-appointed ends,
    And, proudly self-elected,
Crossed the great gulf solo, lowered his sails,
Like some Tyrian trader set up shop
Sans network, sans connection, sans laptop,
"And on the beach undid his corded bales."

To Riccardo Duranti

Vides ut alta stet nive candida Soracte . . .

My friend Riccardo, you are a lucky fellow
To have a hilltop farm in the Sabine hills
Where you raise olives and figs and lettuces
And live with your eager dog and a couple of cats.
A wise man, too, to leave the city behind
And give up teaching down there and work from home,
Translating poems and novels and whatever you like.

You've built an airy new house out of old stone
On the old spot. It's modest, but ample, too,
Fit for your purpose and friendly to visitors.
Even quite ancient things can be put to new use,
Becoming timeless and contemporary.
Conglomerate, limestone, and *sponga* have served you well,
As well as they served your ancestors way back when.

On days when a cool wind combs the leaves of your elms
And ripples your split-by-lightning mulberry,
And the jasmine your mother planted as a girl
Billows and luffs like the hopes of the very young
For whom every season is fresh and the hours move slowly,
As a caravan of clouds casts Salisano
Continually in and out of light and shadow
You can still see, in the distance, Mount Soratte,
Just as the poet did from a different angle
When it was inches taller and covered in snow.

Who needs an apartment in Rome when you have all this?
Who needs to be sipping Giacchè or Amarone
When the *rosso* your cousin Spartaco provides
Comes in huge jugs and gets better the more you drink it?

To Riccardo Duranti

Although I believe this poem should tell you something,
Any advice I might give you would be superfluous;
You're already living the way I would urge you to.
I can only think of a single, trivial warning:
Beware of your nasty old neighbor down the road.
He cheats at pool like a little Berlusconi.

To Barack Obama

You've written me, once again, to ask for money.
I thought I would send you, as well, a little advice,
In nearly perfect confidence it won't reach you.

My father used to exclaim, when one of his children
Was frustrated by human stupidity,
By prejudice, or envy, or petty meanness,
"Don't let the dungheads get you down!" It helped
A bit, perhaps since when he said it, he always
Let loose a hearty belly laugh, in pure
Pleasure at his own sanguine, salty proverb,
Which never left him, however often he found
Occasion to trot it out with his great guffaw,
Even in rather embarrassing circumstances,
As one of my sisters, for instance, was nervously lurching
Off to some tittering rendezvous with her friends
Who were standing there, bewildered, well within hearing.

I imagine you don't. How could you? You wouldn't have time.
For some of us, though, watching all this can be tough,
As much of the country believes you're trouble incarnate,
Mao and Malcolm and Gogmagog rolled into one,
And others are deeply, miserably disappointed
Your presidency has been, of course, imperfect,
And you haven't solved most of our problems the way they'd hoped.
But given the metacrises you were given –
An economy in the tank and two wars on,
With shameless opposition whose loyalties
Attend on their donors and party before their country –
It seems to me so far you've done rather well,
And I think it will look that way in the long perspective
(Poets do take the long view: it's all we've got).

To Barack Obama

And while I have your metaphorical ear,
I thought I would include these rough translations
Of Florentine maxims from the Renaissance:

Too much reliance on a comfort circle
Of loyal friends has scuppered many a prince.

Your enemies are as ruthless as they are foolish
Concerning all the issues that matter most.

The cautious man may miss the safest path.

When you inherit a hopeless enterprise,
Doing the things that might have made a difference
Back when a difference was still there to be made
Doesn't make any difference.

To escape the Cyclops' cave you have to blind him.

This comes to you with only admiration.
You carry an epic burden, and carry it nobly.
Please give my best to Michelle, a wonderful lady.
I'm enclosing, along with this poem, a modest check.

To His Book

You seem to want, my book, to be out on our own,
Imagining the world will be eager to greet you,
Will applaud the panache of your various moods and meters
And ponder the counterpoint of your arrangement.

Children don't listen to parents, or else I would tell you
To temper your expectations, or chuck them entirely.
I doubt you will find yourself dodging the paparazzi,
Or getting invited to all the most glamorous parties,
Or making the short lists. Not that you won't deserve to.
But you're built for distance, not for the sprints to prizes.

My hope for you is that the handful of readers
Who admired your older brothers will like you better,
And another dozen or two will happen across you
And feel compelled to riddle out where you come from.
Everything else is gravy, though welcome, of course.

If they ask you about me, tell them whatever you like.
The truth won't help, and lies won't hurt in the long run.

I know you were hoping for some extravagant send-off.
But at least I didn't compare you to a donkey,
Or a prostitute, or a senile grade-school teacher.

I am not, though, putting this last, where you think it belongs.

✝

To Trebitsch Lincoln in Hell

Where in Hell would Dante Alighieri
Stick you, what torments laced with fire or ice
Would he inflict, how far down would he bury

A connoisseur of almost every vice,
A flimflam man, a thief, a cad, a spy,
A peddler of false hopes and bad advice

Whose penchant for the shameless, bold-faced lie
Consorted with delusional fantasy
From Montreal to Munich to Shanghai

In a career straining credulity,
Who kept on popping up in some odd spot
Like the bad penny of the century

Wherever scoundrels with a half-baked plot
Could cause more trouble, adding your two bits
To further snarl your life tale's tangled knot

Of false identities and nutty fits
And harebrained stunts to plump your empty purse
By conning chumps and chumming up to shits,

Of making dicey situations worse
Through hazardous addiction to foul play
And megalomania? You were a curse

To anyone you met along the way
You took to infamy, whose antics crammed
A bulging Foreign Office dossier

(What clowns you bothered, and what fools you scammed!)
With puzzlement and mounting irritation,
Annoyance typed and scrawled and telegrammed

To Trebitsch Lincoln in Hell

In disbelief and crusty indignation
At squabbles, crimes, political intrigue,
Another hapless passport application,

Caustic dismissals, threats of something big
From a preposterous hallucinating
Sham operator in unlikely league

With fascist thugs and dictators-in-waiting,
Tapping an endless reservoir of schemes
To feed your wounded, vengeful, unabating

Procession of world domination dreams,
Absurd yet dangerous malignancies
Envisioning despicable regimes

In strange alignment, all so you could seize
Power somewhere somehow. Your gall amazes
Anyone who, examining the lees

Of right-wing politics, the clueless mazes
Of failed conspiracies, keeps finding you,
And tracks your progress through its baffling phases:

Born on the Danube, a Hungarian Jew;
Then a failed thespian; a jewel thief;
A fugitive; a journalist; a Lu-

Theran seminarian (this stint was brief);
A missionary who received the call
To carve out and exploit a petty fief

Converting the stubborn Jews of Montreal
(Not one converted), then quit, demanding more
Compensation for your theatrical

To Trebitsch Lincoln in Hell

Evangelizing (if your results were poor,
Your self-regard was only growing greater);
A curate in the parish of Appledore

Terminated rather sooner than later
When you flunked ordination horribly;
A secretary and social investigator

Studying Belgium as the employee
Of your most generous, trusting benefactor,
The cocoa potentate Seebohm Rowntree,

For whom you served as brash and hasty factor,
Brandishing the cause of land reform
To prove a pompous nuisance and bad actor

Badgering functionaries to perform
Unnecessary favors, which got done
Despite resentment fueled by brutal form;

A Liberal MP for Darlington
(Some dogs will have their day, despite their fleas),
Having astonished almost everyone

By nipping the incumbent, H. Pike Pease,
Against the tide, who soon became a joke,
A swaggering backbencher little cheese

Whose accent triggered jibes both times he spoke
(You were irrelevant, but you were loud:
Your vehement posturing managed to provoke

A caricature in *Punch*, which you were proud
To show off from then on, wherever you went),
And under party pressure and a cloud

To Trebitsch Lincoln in Hell

Of soaring debt and wide embarrassment
Was finally persuaded to stand down
After a single year in Parliament

Of meretricious service to both crown
And country (which were *not* free of you yet:
You weren't one to lie low, or just skip town);

A speculator who contrived to get
Investors and East European counts
To back your shifty and untimely bet

On oil bonanzas with quite large amounts
Of capital, despite clear signs of trouble
(Shell companies and vanishing accounts:

Confronting losses, you would always double
Down), at the ill-fated Oil and Drilling Trust
Of Roumania, which rode the next oil bubble

But not for long, then went, predictably, bust,
Leaving you once again in poverty
If somehow free from prosecution, just;

A bald practitioner of forgery,
Signing, when new creditors demanded
A guarantor, the name "Seebohm Rowntree"

To missives of assurance, a trick which landed
You in a little down time, by and by;
A postal censor who got reprimanded

For writing *on* the letters, and in high
Dudgeon at such treatment walked out the door;
A self-denominated "master spy"

To Trebitsch Lincoln in Hell

Trying to work both sides in the Great War
(The Germans nibbled, the Brits would not play ball,
Which left you apoplectic, with a score

To settle with your bête noir, "Blinker" Hall,
A twitch-afflicted naval officer
Who sized your act up and saw through it all

To you, a shameless, fraudulent character
Who'd sold what soul he had, and long ago);
An on the lam shipboard adulterer

Lining up crash pads and, of course, cash flow
In your next stop, New York, where you would try
To peddle your latest dog and pony show,

Poking the hated British in the eye
With scandalous articles and your first book,
Revelations of an International Spy,

Trumpeting treason, which was all it took
To land you, as you preened and celebrated
Celebrity, back, firmly, on the hook

(With a war on, this really could have waited)
Of those fraud charges, cause to extradite
And get you, at long last, incarcerated,

At first in Brooklyn (you put up a fight,
And managed to escape, and then get caught),
Then Parkhurst Prison on the Isle of Wight

For three dull years, a punishment that taught
You absolutely nothing – no restrictions
Could interrupt your fuming, overwrought

To Trebitsch Lincoln in Hell

Propensity for self-propelling fictions,
Which led you off more cliffs, as we shall see;
An ex-con who, with Anglophobe convictions,

Sought restoration of the monarchy
In Germany, and to promote that cause
Courted Prince Wilhelm in the Zuider Zee

(He wouldn't see you); an ally of scofflaws
And militarists intent on snatching power
(That you were Jewish gave these friends some pause)

Like Ludendorff and Erhardt and Max Bauer
And Wolfgang Kapp, who gave the putsch its name
That seized Berlin for a proverbial hour

(Well, five days, really) to abruptly flame
Out in confusion, buckling under the stress
Of crummy players at a dirty game,

And smack dab in the middle of this mess
There *you* were, putting on ridiculous airs
To bully and browbeat the foreign press

As, yes, Director of Foreign Press Affairs,
And as that house of cards began to fall
You did pass Adolf Hitler on the stairs;

A founder of that virulent cabal
Of cancerous revanchist fantasy,
The sinister White International,

A festering wingnut conspiracy
Nursed in Bavaria and Budapest
Committed to fomenting anomie

To Trebitsch Lincoln in Hell

And unifying hatred of the West
That never managed to metastasize,
For all your grotesque zeal and evil zest;

A desperate turncoat, having gotten wise
To plans among your "friends" to snuff you out,
And taken off with a trove of compromis-

Ing documents, which wares you shopped about,
Approaching the French, the English, and the Czechs
With tales of right-wing plotting, which no doubt

Contained exaggerations and complex
Evasions, but for once were basically true,
Though no one would accept those purloined specs

As genuine, because they came from you;
An aid to *Chinese* forces of reaction,
Advisor to Yang Sen and Wu P'ei-fu

And other warlords of the Chihli faction,
Who guided a fund-raising carnival
To Europe on their behalf (which gained no traction);

An arms dealer, perhaps; a professional
Gambler, who thought he knew a way to win
At baccarat (you didn't); a tell-all

Purveyor of your heroics (this had worn thin);
The blessed recipient of revelation
At the Astor House Hotel in Tientsin,

Who then embraced "the great renunciation"
And "quit the world" (just momentarily)
In search of spiritual elevation,

To Trebitsch Lincoln in Hell

And, after a brief fling with Theosophy,
Retreated to a Buddhist monastery
On Ceylon, where, in proud humility,

You contemplated truth; a missionary
And roving lecturer raptly expounding
Buddhist doctrine to various unwary

Audiences, somehow involved in founding
A center for enlightenment in San
Francisco (thought the first); again confounding

All expectation, a certified holy man,
Having gone through initiation rites
To be branded and ordained at Pao-hua Shan,

Near Nanking, who ascended greater heights,
Quickly clambering up another rung
From monk to *Bodhisattva*, and by such lights

You were henceforth the Venerable Chao Kung;
The self-appointed Abbot of Shanghai,
After returning from yet one more far-flung

Soul-fishing expedition with disci-
Ples (thirteen, to be precise, believe it or not)
Who found themselves soon dominated by

This strangely charismatic polyglot
Angry tyrannical delusionist,
Who sucked them dry, and blew his stack, a lot;

An unabashed early apologist
For Japanese hegemony, who pleaded
That subjugation to an imperialist

To Trebitsch Lincoln in Hell

Superior race was just what China needed;
An advocate of world peace, whose demand
All governments resign, now, went unheeded;

The incubator of one final grand
Weird fantasy of global domination,
Whose overtures to Nazi High Command

With plans to start your own broadcasting station
For German propaganda in Tibet
Included offering a demonstration,

Once granted the requested tête-à-tête,
Your powers were vast and supernatural,
Claiming the moment you and Hitler met

Three wise men would emerge out of the wall
(This epochal entente was not to be);
A corpse at Shanghai General Hospital

On 6 October 1943.
How in the world did you pull all this off?
You must have had some disarming quality

To squirm your way to new trough after trough,
Some charm, some dazzle, plus tenacity:
Your enemies could fret and swear and scoff

At your inveterate ubiquity
But you would show them they weren't done with you,
Or you with them. Some bipolarity

Seems more than likely, for you cycled through
Your visionary highs and blacked-out lows
(Those lies were lies, but you believed them, too)

To Trebitsch Lincoln in Hell

As you aspired then plummeted then rose
In brilliant self-esteem then crashed and burned.
When your bizarre career drew to its close,

When oblivion faded and consciousness returned
And you found you were just another shade,
What dismal form of misery had you earned

With all the fuss you'd caused and mess you'd made?
When hideous Minos wrapped his horrid tail
Around himself, what devastating grade

Did he assign *your* life beyond the pale,
Assessing peccancy in bad events
Comprising your long compromising tale?

Not to the Circles of Incontinence,
Though you were qualified to share the pain,
With mistresses on several continents,

Of spirits buffeted by the hurricane
That drives and pounds the Lustful; or to lie
Helpless beneath the freezing, filthy rain

That soaks the howling Gluttons; or to cry
Along with the Avaricious and Prodigal
Circling in fruitless labor, as they try

To push huge weights with just their chests, and all
Collide together with a wrenching thud,
Turn, and slog back to stalemate; or to brawl

Among the Wrathful, coated in the crud
Of the River Styx; or, with the Sullen, sprawl
Face-downward, gurgling in its stinking mud.

To Trebitsch Lincoln in Hell

Not to the plain inside the buttressed wall
Of Dis, where, baked in flaming sepulchers,
The Heretics forever writhe and call

Out in convulsions, or where the Squanderers
Scramble in panic through the dreary wood
To stumble, caught and rent by packs of curs,

Though as a penal candidate you could
Fall either place, roasting or ripped to bits,
Were you not bound for a worse neighborhood.

Not even the steeply terraced torture pits
Of Malebolge would suit your foulest crime,
Though several of them wouldn't be bad fits,

Since Fraudulence you worked at, and full-time:
The First, where hornèd demons with long scourges
Lash the Seducers; the Seventh, where the slime

Of snakes joins that of Thieves, and what emerges
Is both and neither, a swallowing embrace
That fuses, morphs, and splits, then reconverges

As man and devouring serpent interlace
To slither from different creatures to the same,
Four limbs, two heads, one tail, one trunk, one face;

The Eighth, where clothed in all-consuming flame
The Fraudulent Counselors turn incinerated;
The Ninth, where in excruciating shame

The Sowers of Scandal and Schism get mutilated
In endless cycles, healing while reeling back
To suffer the sword of the demon designated

To Trebitsch Lincoln in Hell

To slash them back asunder with a hack,
Lopping a limb off here, a head off there,
Carving another open from mouth to crack;

The Tenth, the lowest and most awful, where,
Bloated and dropsical, the Falsifiers
Rot, wailing in the putrefying air,

Impersonators, Counterfeiters, Liars
All swollen, warped, tumescent. No, the dark
Logic of Dantesque punishment requires

Your classification by your blackest mark.
You must go all the way down, where Hell craters
Into the bitter, bone-chilling, and stark

Gelid extremes that freeze the wretched Traitors,
To Antenora, from whose glacial lake
The heads of those infernal calculators

Who turn against their homeland jut and quake,
Chattering in unending agony,
Or, miserable, to motionlessly ache

In terminal Judecca, where you'd be
Fastened, encased from head to toe in ice
Like a wisp of straw in glass, for treachery

To benefactors. There you would pay the price
For crimes that didn't, were retribution so
Ordered and allegorically precise.

Would your crimes were the worst we came to know.

Sky Burial

    Wherever the soul goes,
On top of the world the body is broken and eaten.
    For three ceremonial days
   It is washed in scented water, tended
    By monks, while the soul stays,
Roaming the body, confused (on what threshold who knows?),
     Bereft and grieving,
   And, as it lingers, is read to
  From *The Tibetan Book of the Dead*, to
    Soften and sweeten
   Its trauma, and guide its leaving.
    Then, all that ended,

    The soul having departed,
They crumple the empty body, snapping its back
   To fold it up quite small,
  And take it, on a palanquin,
   To the sky burial
Plateau, where, with an art that seems cold-hearted
    To other cultures,
   Gutted, flesh chopped bite-sized,
  Skull and brains smashed, bones pulverized
    And mixed with yak
   Butter, it's fed to the vultures
    Now crowding in,

Sky Burial

   Summoned, for centuries,
By windings of the sky-horn, and a fire
   Of juniper twigs, to eat
 The mortal parts of everyone,
   Our organs, gristle, meat.
These emanations of white *dakinis*
     Assimilate
   And raise us, even dying
 In upper atmosphere, as, flying
    Ever higher,
   They disarticulate
    In wind and sun.

Hearing Voices

Whose voice is this, just audible through static?
Crinkled and interrupted, to be sure,
But, even though the medium's impure,
Hypnotic, orotund, and automatic,

The grumbling baritone of Tennyson
Reciting, again, "The Charge of the Light Brigade"
As wave on wave the syllables crest and fade:
"*Some* one had *blun*der'd," as they'd often done.

And whose is this? Pitched in a higher key,
The almost Bostonian, tartly nasal "a"
Accenting what the good man had to say
To fellow citizens, robustly free,

Speaking in words, no chanting metronome
Of golden phrases from the treasure vault,
But idiosyncratic Uncle Walt
Just talking to us, smiling and at home

In his "America." The primitive
Technology that Edison invented
Captured articulations represented
As paraffin and beeswax let them live,

Echoing down to ears in distant ages
(Like hopeful capsules launched far into space
To signal someone we're the human race)
The voices fallen silent on their pages.

King Lear

Of course some wise guy *would* nickname him "King,"
That Princeton rookie with his college ring
Pitching for Cincinnati, who finished last.
He couldn't hit, or run, or throw it fast,
And didn't binge or brawl or anything,
Just floated a knuckleball they swung right past.

A player's tale: the spotlight of renown
Switched off, you're yesterday's ticket, out of town
And back to Charles. He hurt his arm next year
And he was gone like luck, or penny beer.
And when an old man's mourners set him down
In wind and rain, who knew he was King Lear?

✣

Hamlet

It's quiet here. A stoic rectitude
Props up the weather-pummeled citizens,
Craggy yet almost cheerful. Uniform
Gray granite cottages, precipitous
And sturdy, make the most of things. The wind
Does all the talking hereabouts, and who
Would think to think about the universe?
Their certainties define them, not their doubts.

✝

Ice Age Art

Fashioned by firelight, nicked and scooped and planed
By crude flint burins nibbed to scrape and hone
Till something like a miracle remained
On bone and antler, ivory and stone,

Where hours of pinpoint labor left behind,
Faithful to details of anatomy,
First inklings of the panoramic mind
In polished, miniature menagerie,

The animals that peopled their stark scene
Of snow drift, barren, glacial watercourse
(Bison, musk ox, mammoth, wolverine,
Cave bear, cave lion, reindeer, ibex, horse)

Hardened to artifact in action poses
(Galloping, swimming, leaping onto prey):
Paleolithic artwork presupposes,
For subsequent endeavors to this day,

Compulsions to creation that inform
Signs of the origin – there at the start
To mine the world to mime the world, and form
The ur-fidelities of Ice Age art.

Fidelities

Whatever piece of code,
Hard-wired millennia, dictates they cross
   The Himalayan chain
To reach their distant wintertime abode,
   Reliving all the strain
Of their monumental journey's struggle and loss,
   The graceful Demoiselle Crane,

Anthropoides virgo,
Slender and beautiful, known by its white
   Ear tufts and long black breast
Plume, seems too frail to, year after driven year, go
   On such an arduous quest,
Scaling those glacial summits in its flight,
   Then crossing back to nest

In marshes on the steppes,
Where their peculiar courtship rituals
   Require elaborate
Wing-flaps, and bows, and odd, balletic steps,
   As they communicate
In long duets, coordinating calls
   To single out a mate

For life. Fidelity
So perfect moved Valmiki (so goes the tale)
   By the Tamasa Stream,
Who saw a loving couple suddenly
   Divide like a ripped seam
Split when a hunter's arrow felled the male,
   And heard the female scream

Fidelities

In her bewildered grief,
And felt his anger surge spontaneously
  To sharpen to a curse
Wishing the killer unrest without relief:
  The world's first man-made verse,
In a form of metrical dexterity
  Whole epics would rehearse.

  Metapoetic birds,
The *Koonj* (from *kraunch*, like "crane") can represent
  Feminine loveliness
In delicately curved dimensions words
  Take figures to finesse,
Or those whose wanderings of long extent
  Their journeyings express

  Through parallel's conceit,
For what exhausted traveler, far from home,
  Looking for one small source
Of strength or hope, would not admire their feat
  Of pluck and subtle force,
Braving the altitudes to overcome
  The hazards of the course?

  (Fatigue, hunger, predation
Defeat the laboring heart's heroic rallies
  Every difficult day:
In the length of each biannual migration
  Thousands will drop away.)
We know now that they don't cut through the valleys,
  But somehow fight their way

Fidelities

    Right up to clear the top
Of ridges as high as 26,000 feet,
    Riding the thermals so
They elevate (it's death to start to stop)
    Above sheer ice and snow
To hit, head on, the big winds, beat and beat
    Against the blast, then go

    Over at last to glide
Downward on resting wings, till some prenatal
    Instinct decides it's time
To turn their faces toward the great divide
    And, in formation, climb
To meet the wind-tormented, often fatal
    Precincts of the sublime.

Harrison's Clock

Even the most recalcitrant conundrum,
Most enigmatic brain-teaser, most baffling,
    Perplexedly stupefying
  And dilemmatic quandary,
      Logic-defying,
Which brings our rut-inhabiting and humdrum
    Intelligence to some
  Impenetrable boundary,
Some blind spot, some unfathomable sum
      And sets us waffling,
  Imprisoned by polarities
(Nature or nurture? particle or wave?),
    Some cul-de-sac or cave
  Murky with deep obscurities

– Dark energy, dark matter, neutrino mass,
Cantor's infinities, Schrödinger's cat,
    The source of gamma rays,
  The seven bridges of Königsberg,
      The intricate "maze
Of moral relativism" (or turf, or grass,
    Or maize), a better mousetrap,
  The IT nightmare of Rube Goldberg
Data base management, an honest house trap
      Repair, a fat-
  Free diet that satisfies, the sins
Of fathers visiting yet one more time,
    The perfect, victimless crime,
  The origin of origins –

Yields sometimes, in the end, not to the flights
Of fancy speculation, sidereal charts,
    Or the pure good of theory,
  But to the dull, mechanical,
        Patient and weary
Labors of tedious days and troubled nights
    Through trials that fail and fail,
  Obsession's grim, tyrannical
Absorption in the pickiest detail,
        The stubborn arts
  Of the compulsive, focused will,
Accepting the perfectionist's confinement
      In quest of what refinement
  Can amplify her growing skill:

For instance, the holy grail of navigation,
Discovering one's longitude at sea,
    Which vexed such intellects
  As Newton, Halley, Euler, Hooke,
        And caused the wrecks
Of countless ships (one horrid illustration:
    Their reckoning off by miles
  Despite procedures by the book,
Two thousand sailors died on the Scilly Isles,
      A tragedy
  That spurred the fabled Longitude Act,
Establishing a monetary prize
      Of unprecedented size
  For any reasonably exact

Solution), was found not by ephemerides
Like Galileo's, or Flamsteed's catalog
    Mapping celestial motion,
  Or any correction for the flux
        Of trackless ocean
Using the stars and moon as luminous guides,
    Or more unlikely helps
  Proposed to resolve the fiendish crux,
Like timing the pathetic howls and yelps
        Of a tortured dog
  Using "powder of sympathy,"
Or stationing ships with guns to fire away
    Appointed times of day
  At intervals across the sea,

But a self-taught provincial, an abrupt,
Obscure clock-maker, one John Harrison,
    Whose artistry reformed
  The craft of the chronometric trade,
        As he transformed
The laggard clock, forever interrupt-
    Ed by wear and winding, fall-
  Ing out of time, to a home-made
Baroque high-tech device precise past all
        Comparison,
  Equipped to counteract the raw
Conditions (changes in humidity,
    Temperature, gravity,
  And barometric pressure, the yaw

Harrison's Clock

And pitch of shipboard, the insidious
Corrosion of salt air, each variable
    Conducive to mistakes)
  By carpentry taking in hand
      Clamps, scrapers, stakes,
Tongs, saws, screw arbors with fastidious
    Mastery, calibrated
  By innovation on demand
Of all the staggering gadgets he created,
    Very able
  To rig up what he needed – pairing
Brass and steel in the bi-metallic strip,
    Countering friction's grip
  By inventing the ball bearing,

Plus other gifts he found just feeling his way,
The gridiron pendulum, the grasshopper
    Escapement, lubrication
  Via lignum vitae – to mechanize
      Close calculation
In his great sea clocks' brilliant brass display
    Of balance and precision,
  Of whirring wheels that harmonize
With rods and springs and dials in timely vision,
    Each show-stopper
  Proving, as Hogarth said, "one of
The most exquisite movements ever made,"
    A spectacular cascade
  Unwinding long labors of love

(Love of the object, true – true love of art,
Of tiny fillips no one else will see,
    Of ornamental function
   Fusing resistant elements
      In taut conjunction
Of form with force and shimmering part with part),
    "H1," the toast of all
  London, "H2," which represents
Breakthrough minute adjustments, most of all
     "Harrison 3,"
  The master's "curious third machine,"
An odd assembly of balances and gears
    That cost him nineteen years
  To streamline, till, lighter and lean,

Comprising seven hundred and fifty-three
Separate parts, it too sat in its box,
    Polished and perfected
  Only, just like the other two,
     To be rejected
By its creator, and never go to sea,
    When Harrison decided
  A fantastic pocket watch would do,
If built along the principles that guided
     The three sea clocks,
  Even better once put to the test
By the Board of Longitude's adjudication
    Of Parliament's stipulation
  For success, a voyage to the West

Harrison's Clock

Indies, on which the watch, "Harrison 4,"
Its miniaturized machinery
    Sheer jewel, ruby pins
  And diamond pallets cut so fine
      The tiny ins
And outs of wheel and lever have all the more
    Capacity to amaze,
  Performed superbly right down the line,
Losing a mere five seconds in eighty-one days,
    Though chicanery
  Orchestrated by wily Nevil
Maskelyne, a biased, contrarian,
    Committed Lunarian
  Who was Harrison's personal devil,

Succeeded in denying him the Prize
On a bureaucratic technicality
    (Royal intervention
  Was necessary to reward
      The man's invention
And, after trial and torment, recognize
    That the watch could, in fact,
  Although the Board was not on board,
Within the clear requirements of the Act
    Keep time at sea),
  While all three clocks got commandeered
By Maskelyne, in order to be "tested,"
    Suddenly, rudely wrested
  From a man he both despised and feared

Harrison's Clock

To be trundled over cobbles, disrespected,
Manhandled, dropped, and ultimately ruled
    Failures, then locked away
  By their peevish, petty enemy,
    To rust and decay
In a damp closet, dirty, unwound, neglected,
    Dismissed by jealous slander,
  To wait for more than a century
Until the labors of Lieutenant Commander
    Rupert T. Gould
  (Who toiled, unpaid, a dozen years
On painstaking and meticulous restoration,
    In service to the nation,
  Of mainspring barrels, winding gears,

And steel check-pieces on the balance springs)
Would reconstruct their works and set them right
    And running, to this day,
  In Flamsteed House, where, venerated,
    On bright array,
They are marveled at as timeless, beautiful things,
    Even "H3," which seems
  To stand ("not merely complicated,
It is abstruse") for art that risks extremes
    To keep, despite
  Each disappointment and hard knock,
Despite the machinations of rival schools
    And telling deafness of fools,
  Pitch perfect time, like Harrison's clock.

Shakespeare's Horse

He was a man knew horses, so we moved
As wills were one, and all was won at will,
In hand with such sleight handling as improved
Those parks and parcels where we're racing still,

Pounding like pairs of hooves or pairs of hearts
Through woodland scenes and lush, dramatic spaces,
With all our parts in play to play all parts
In pace with pace to put us through his paces.

Ages have passed. All channels channel what
Imagined these green plots and gave them names
Down to the smallest role, if and and but,
What flies the time (the globe gone up in flames),

What thunders back to ring the ringing course
And runs like the streaking will, like Shakespeare's horse.

A Note About the Author

Photo courtesy of Rob Crandall © 2014

Joseph Harrison was born in Richmond, Virginia, grew up in Virginia and Alabama, and studied at Yale and Johns Hopkins. His first book of poems, *Someone Else's Name* (Waywiser, 2003), was chosen as one of five poetry books of the year by the *Washington Post*. He was awarded an Academy Award in Literature by the American Academy of Arts and Letters in 2005. A second book of poetry, *Identity Theft*, was published by Waywiser in 2008. In 2009 he received a fellowship in poetry from the Guggenheim Foundation. He lives in Baltimore, Maryland, with his wife, Carla Harrison.

Other Books from Waywiser

POETRY

Al Alvarez, *New & Selected Poems*
Chris Andrews, *Lime Green Chair*
George Bradley, *A Few of Her Secrets*
Geoffrey Brock, *Voices Bright Flags*
Robert Conquest, *Blokelore & Blokesongs*
Robert Conquest, *Penultimata*
Morri Creech, *Field Knowledge*
Morri Creech, *The Sleep of Reason*
Peter Dale, *One Another*
Erica Dawson, *Big-Eyed Afraid*
B. H. Fairchild, *The Art of the Lathe*
David Ferry, *On This Side of the River: Selected Poems*
Jeffrey Harrison, *The Names of Things: New & Selected Poems*
Joseph Harrison, *Identity Theft*
Joseph Harrison, *Someone Else's Name*
Joseph Harrison, ed., *The Hecht Prize Anthology, 2005-2009*
Anthony Hecht, *Collected Later Poems*
Anthony Hecht, *The Darkness and the Light*
Carrie Jerrell, *After the Revival*
Stephen Kampa, *Bachelor Pad*
Rose Kelleher, *Bundle o' Tinder*
Mark Kraushaar, *The Uncertainty Principle*
Matthew Ladd, *The Book of Emblems*
Dora Malech, *Shore Ordered Ocean*
Eric McHenry, *Potscrubber Lullabies*
Eric McHenry and Nicholas Garland, *Mommy Daddy Evan Sage*
Timothy Murphy, *Very Far North*
Ian Parks, *Shell Island*
V. Penelope Pelizzon, *Whose Flesh is Flame, Whose Bone is Time*
Chris Preddle, *Cattle Console Him*
Shelley Puhak, *Guinevere in Baltimore*
Christopher Ricks, ed., *Joining Music with Reason:*
34 Poets, British and American, Oxford 2004-2009
Daniel Rifenburgh, *Advent*
Mary Jo Salter, *It's Hard to Say: Selected Poems*
W. D. Snodgrass, *Not for Specialists: New & Selected Poems*
Mark Strand, *Almost Invisible*
Mark Strand, *Blizzard of One*
Bradford Gray Telford, *Perfect Hurt*
Matthew Thorburn, *This Time Tomorrow*
Cody Walker, *Shuffle and Breakdown*
Deborah Warren, *The Size of Happiness*

Other Books from Waywiser

Clive Watkins, *Already the Flames*
Clive Watkins, *Jigsaw*
Richard Wilbur, *Anterooms*
Richard Wilbur, *Mayflies*
Richard Wilbur, *Collected Poems 1943-2004*
Norman Williams, *One Unblinking Eye*
Greg Williamson, *A Most Marvelous Piece of Luck*

FICTION
Gregory Heath, *The Entire Animal*
Mary Elizabeth Pope, *Divining Venus*
K. M. Ross, *The Blinding Walk*
Gabriel Roth, *The Unknowns**
Matthew Yorke, *Chancing It*

ILLUSTRATED
Nicholas Garland, *I wish ...*
Eric McHenry and Nicholas Garland, *Mommy Daddy Evan Sage*

NON-FICTION
Neil Berry, *Articles of Faith: The Story of British Intellectual Journalism*
Mark Ford, *A Driftwood Altar: Essays and Reviews*
Richard Wollheim, *Germs: A Memoir of Childhood*

* Co-published with Picador